the future of the soul
2012 & the global shift in consciousness

ian lawton
with janet treloar, hazel newton & tracey robins

Rational Spirituality Press

First published in 2010 by Rational Spirituality Press.

All enquiries to be directed to www.rspress.org.

A CIP catalogue record for this title is available from the British Library.

ISBN 978-0-9549176-6-1

Cover design by Ian Lawton.
Cover image by Jason Waskey (www.jasonwaskey.com).
Ian Lawton photograph by James Franklin (www.jamesfranklin.com).

Printed and bound by Henry Ling Limited, Dorchester, England.

Although this book was always planned, its actual contents came about by one of those great synchronicities that those on a spiritual path learn to recognize and embrace.

It began on the evening of 4th March 2010 at Gaunts House, north of Wimborne, Dorset. I was a student attending a training module with the Past Life Regression Academy, run with a wonderful mixture of professionalism, integrity, spirituality and love by Andy Tomlinson and Hazel Newton. They always try to have some sort of evening activity or entertainment to help us unwind, because the days are pretty intense and high energy. Lots of personal issues come to the surface in our regressions, which is part of the learning process, but also ensures we've got rid of our own emotional baggage before we start acting as therapists to others.

On the first evening Hazel had agreed to guide one of the assistant trainers, Janet Treloar, into an altered state so that she could act as a channel for any energies from the light realms who might want to answer questions about 2012 and the global shift in consciousness. This is a technique not totally dissimilar to the one that Andy and I had used in *The Wisdom of the Soul*, although Janet is such an excellent trance subject that little induction is required. But it was hardly an exercise of the same rigor, because Hazel, myself and another assistant trainer, Tracey Robins, only had twenty minutes or so to prepare our questions. So we had no great confidence that they would yield significant results, and at the outset were really treating the whole thing as a bit of fun.

Yet as the session unfolded it became clear that we were witnessing something that was both powerful and important. Ever since she was small Janet has been open to the spirit world, but she soon learned to control and even repress this. She has never channeled on a regular basis, the previous time being about a year before during the same training module, but apparently even that had been very low key by comparison.

From the outset she began shaking from head to toe, and this continued throughout the hour-long session. Afterwards she said it felt like 'something about twenty feet long was trying to fit into my body', although half way through the first energy left and another even larger one came in. In fact as observers we all noticed a temporary respite in her shaking at this point.

What's more, not only was Janet showing channeling talents she hadn't fully tapped into before, but the messages coming through her were hugely positive and uplifting, yet still grounded. This is exactly what I'd been searching for, because the channeled offerings about 2012 and beyond I'd come across previously seemed to veer between doom-laden warnings of catastrophe on the one hand, and sugar-coated messages of spiritual ascension for 'the chosen ones' on the other. At the end of the session we all just looked at each other and said 'wow'!

We quickly realized that the wonderful messages we were being blessed with should be explored further and then delivered to a global audience as soon as possible. And the timing was surely no coincidence, given that I'd already been planning for my next book to be on exactly these topics. So I sorted the material into a number of main headings, and created a whole new set of detailed questions within each, designed to clarify and expand on the information we'd already received. Hazel and Tracey provided input to this process but Janet was deliberately left out.

The four of us met again for our second session on Easter Sunday, the 4th April, at Hazel's flat in

Bristol. We were full of excitement and anticipation, sensing that the possibilities for gaining incredible insights and information were limited only by our own intellects and imagination. And as I put the questions to our sources over a lengthy session that lasted more than four hours, they didn't disappoint.

The major difference this time was that we were communicating with many more energies, and most of them tended to concentrate themselves in Janet's head area rather than entering her whole body. The exception was a small, rather excitable but totally delightful 'nature spirit' energy, who initially occupied her right shoulder but caused it to twitch so violently it was painful. When we had to ask him to calm down he moved into her legs, which in turn began to twitch, but thankfully less painfully.

To turn to the process itself, the quality of any channeled messages always depends not only on the wisdom of the source or sources themselves, of which more shortly, but also on the extent to which the human channel can 'get out of the way'. Indeed a 'clear channel' like Janet can remove themselves completely:

I take myself off to my 'safe place', which is under an oak tree in a meadow. When I invite the highest sources available to literally step into me I give them permission to use my body and energy. So I try as much as possible to remain under that tree so my consciousness doesn't inhibit them using my mind and voice to process and convey the information they choose to share with us.

This method obviously works because, speaking from the experience of listening to the many, many hours of trance sessions conducted as research for *The Wisdom of the Soul*, there appears to be very little if any conscious interference in her transmissions. This is especially demonstrated by the delivery of her responses being relatively fast, with few hesitations. Indeed she was still flowing just as quickly and easily at the end of our four-hour second session as she did at the beginning.

Moreover virtually all the material received has been deemed useful and relevant, and therefore included in this book, with omissions mainly consisting of duplication between the two sessions. Admittedly I've often tweaked her spoken words to produce the transcriptions that follow, but this is only in terms of order, grammar, repetition and so on, to ensure they're as clear and concise as possible. Also the order of the first set of transmissions has been changed in places to fit into the major headings that were only developed subsequently. In each section the material from each session is presented in order to provide the best narrative flow for the reader. Occasionally explanatory notes have been added in square brackets.

As for the possibility that Janet was merely regurgitating previously acquired information, she has read some books about 2012, but much of what follows isn't found in or even contradicts their contents. In particular as far as historical information is concerned, she reports that she knows Jesus was born around 2000 years ago but very little from before that time – for example about earlier civilizations, or about global and human evolution in general.

In any case, by contrast to my normal approach to evidence under the banner of what I refer to as 'Rational Spirituality', this whole exercise was never designed to be rigorous and evidential. The sources we were working with weren't concerned with verifiable, low level information like 'what is my mother's name' or 'what was my grandfather's profession', although they probably could have got it if we'd pushed them. Indeed as you read through the interchanges you will see that we deliberately kept our questions at a relatively high level throughout, and didn't ask for undue detail. Some may see this as a weakness, but the reality is that the strongest message to come through was that the future of life on planet earth is by no means fixed. So it's pointless to ask detailed questions because the answer, if it's genuine and not consciously influenced, will tend to be 'it depends'.

In particular we didn't ask for details of exactly where future natural upheavals might occur. This is because, even if the information *was* accurate, it could only induce potential panic that would be entirely nonproductive – once you understand the proper spiritual context of such events, which will be explained in due course.

Despite its length, after our second session Janet was still semi 'tuned in'. And during these further discussions our sources did deliberate over whether they could give us details of a definitive event in the immediate future to prove their credibility. But because of the danger that free will might invalidate any prediction, we tended to see this more as a potential hindrance than a help. In fact she did receive a flash of some major political event in Russia, which we didn't pursue. Imagine our chagrin when exactly a week later the Polish president was killed in an air crash over Smolensk, and she knew this was exactly what they had been trying to show her.

Despite this we all still feel that the main thing with channeled material is to see if the information resonates with you, and if it does you just have to trust your sources. Of course you can ask them who they are. Indeed we did, and they said we could refer to them as 'the council', a large and fluid group that represents various aspects of our part of the universe. But such assurances of identity don't *prove* much, if anything, because if your sources are 'jokers in the pack' they're not going to admit as much, they're going to tell you that they're the 'masters of the universe' or some such.

Nevertheless, if you trust your sources we would suggest that it's preferable to be dealing with a group such as this, because they can bring in the relevant 'expert' to answer questions on a particular topic. By contrast single sources can have a more limited and sometimes biased perspective.

The one control we did think we could usefully employ was to send the draft manuscript to our friend and colleague Toni Winninger in the US, so that she could cross-check its contents with the 'Masters' that she has been successfully channeling for some years now. She kindly responded with support and a few items of clarification. But when we asked our own sources whether we should also follow what we understood to be normal protocol, that is reading back the final manuscript to them so they could check it for accuracy, their response was somewhat unexpected:

> *We can give you information, but part of the process is that you resonate with it and put down what you feel will resonate with others. You will be able to judge that far better than us.*

Indeed this is illustrative of the many apparently counterintuitive responses they gave us. They immediately felt more resonant than the response we might have expected, even though we are all fairly used to using our soul rather than human perspective. All of which – to us at least, and hopefully to you as well – lends a greater air of authenticity to these messages.

The four of us have found that the process of putting this book together has really accelerated our own energies. The more we've switched on to the possibilities of the shift, the more we've seen that the same expansive, positive attitudes found in the council's messages are actually everywhere we look. And we've realized just how many people really are waking up, and just how quickly. So on all levels we're hugely, hugely thankful to the various energies on the council for sharing their wonderful insights, and for allowing us to be involved in this process.

The next few years will contain much change and some hardship. But if these messages are right, and the four of us feel they most likely are, we should all be incredibly excited about an opportunity we've all been planning for and eagerly awaiting for literally thousands of years...

Ian Lawton
April 2010

the nature of our sources

You have regularly used the term 'council' to describe yourselves. Can you tell us more about this?

It's a very human word. It just means a collective group of different consciousnesses that are from many different levels, places and species. It involves everything to do with earth, but also outside of earth as well, so the council is huge.

[The remaining information in this section was obtained from Janet when still 'tuned in' after our second session.]

How many souls are on the council?

A good few hundred, if not more because there are more in the background that come in at certain times. They are covering so many bases. There are lots of souls from other places and dimensions, and everything on earth is represented, the elemental kingdom, the human kingdom, the animal kingdom. Council is the term they use, but it's not a hard and fast thing, they bring different souls in for different things. They've learned this time so they bring in advice from new groups as and when they need it, for example to find out information 'on the ground' from people who have just left earth. There is a group from Haiti with the council now, and they are checking how the earth feels in these places.

What kind of souls are on the council?

Our part of the universe is like a cube that overlaps with others. The only soul we spoke to today who is involved with more than just our 'bit' was the 'helper of Source' [who talked to us about the last shift]. He actually dates back to the Big Bang and even the universe before that.

the background to the current shift

What can you tell us about the shifts taking place on planet earth at this time?

All this has been going on for a long time. The shift started around a hundred years ago, but has really accelerated in the last ten years, and will culminate in the next seven. So while the majority of people will now actually see and feel the shift, it's been happening anyway, in the molecules throughout the body, shifting and changing throughout the generations, which is why you can now work consciously in this higher vibration. And the changes are not just across this planet but across many, many planets.

What will we actually experience?

The twitching you can see in her [Janet's] body is an intensified version of how the vibrations of the molecules will actually change and shift. But this will be a slower process than people think. People will just get naturally used to it, just become attuned to it.

Is that everybody?

In every living thing. It's working throughout and there'll be other things that people can see through this as it changes. Things that aren't clear at the moment to the naked eye will be. And the shift and change has to happen naturally for people to accept what they're seeing, and to believe what they're seeing.

SESSION 2

[The first energy we made contact with in the second session later revealed that they were heavily involved in the last shift.]

What proportion of the souls currently incarnated on earth are from other planets?

About an eighth.

How long have they been coming in for?

It's been increasing. It started sixty, seventy years ago. There's more now than there has been.

Is there anything else you would like to tell us about the background to the current shift?

Different cultures and different places have been awakened at different times. You live in a global world, technology has increased so you can take in what's happening all around the world at once. Things have had to change this time, one place cannot increase without the other, it's an amalgamation. And special attention was given to the West as it had not been awoken before, and it had to be done in a way that those people would accept. It was done more slowly and with a lot more difficulty than in other places.

Is this because it hadn't really happened here in the West before?

Minds were too set. There is a pack mentality that is not talked about. Those that were different were not necessarily accepted. But there were souls who chose that particular experimental route, and by speaking their truth many did battle against the tide. And it all helped, it just took longer than we expected. It's still not at the level it needs to be at now, which is why everything is increasing to such a degree.

So are things being accelerated now?

Yes. Extra help is being given, just like we are doing here with you. We've had to adapt to a mindset in the West that we weren't used to. Our help might not be in the way we would have originally chosen, but it is working. For example, we are aware of the way people worship 'celebrities' in the West, often more than they do religious or political figures, and we have used that to bring about much knowledge and awakening. Many celebrities are waking up other souls in their own right, through mediums that the West will accept.

So you've had to be flexible, but are you happy with the progress now being made?

Yes, we are happy. We are just surprised at how much we have had to adapt and change over the last few years, but it's all coming together now.

the last shift

Has this happened before?

Yes, some 20,000 to 30,000 years ago in your terms.

What was the outcome then?

They didn't cope so well. Their bodies weren't as dense as they are now, and souls merged together and did things they really shouldn't. It was decided they should leave for a while, and have experiences in other places before coming back to earth. So many of them are trying this experience of an energy shift for a second time now.

And this time nothing is set in stone. That's the beauty of this experience, and why the whole galaxy is watching it. Never before has this been done, where the outcome is not certain.

SESSION 2

Can you tell us more about the last shift?

We are happy to talk about that, we have people that were there. It was a different time on earth, the goals were different. Souls wanted to learn about expansion. They already knew quite a lot, and they had the ability to change the form of their bodies as and when was needed. But they were learning about expansion outside of the body too, and even a removal of their energy out and then back in. Perhaps it happened too quickly. We thought they could cope better.

So did they have physical bodies?

Yes, but to different degrees. Some were denser than others. Those that could lead lives away from other souls could remain quite fluid in form, but the more they encountered other souls the more solid their form needed to be to remain separate. As long as they remained apart from the rest of society, even in groups that were on the same level, they knew how to keep themselves separate from each other. But, just like you see in cities now, when there is a closeness a natural soul energy exchange happens. And that can become very confusing once different personalities are in the mix, because some will naturally take and some will naturally give.

Previously you mentioned souls merging when they weren't supposed to. Is this what you're referring to now?

No, all this was before the energy shift. There was a difference between people already. We expected the expansion would be in those with more fluid bodies, but the dominant forms that emerged were those with the denser bodies. They were the ones that remained, and this is your lineage.

So could the denser people see the less physical people?

They could, but as the shift progressed it became more difficult for them. Those in the dense bodies used the increased energy to their own ends. Those with the more fluid bodies used the energy to leave, they didn't want to be a part of it. They had lived as part of a society together for a long time but the differences became too great, so they chose to leave.

Is there any similarity in the differences between the various types of people then and those that are emerging this time round?

Then you could see the differences with the naked eye, now you can't. That's why you need to see more with your heart than your eyes.

Why is it different this time round?

Last time we thought souls would come together even with their differences. That they would help each other, and enjoy the expansion together and use it wisely. This time there is a far greater capacity to help one another, to help those who aren't seeing to see. The memories of before are in all our souls. They are very deep and no one wants what happened before to happen again this time.

When did all this happen?

It's part of the 26,000 year cycle that is easy to find reference to in your culture now. [This is discussed more in the next section.]

Whereabouts was the human population concentrated on the earth 26,000 years ago?

Near the equator. The way the earth was then the climate had more extremes, and human life was most comfortable nearer the equator. Nearer to the poles there was very little life at all. The most evolved souls were right on top of the equator.

Can you give us an idea of the level of culture they had in those days? What was their most sophisticated technology, for example?

Their technology utilized the power of their minds. Some created purely with their minds, but almost had to dedicate their whole lives to doing this, and to separating themselves off. But more and more these people used what the earth had given them to create, and they involved their minds more, a skill which has since been forgotten.

Can you explain what you mean by 'create'? Create what?

Create comfortable places to live. Create sources of sustenance, food and drink.

Do you mean they could literally create a building or some food from nothing?

They could find sources of water, for example, and they knew how to adapt them to their bodies just by thinking. So if there was an impurity within the water they would be able to find out and remove it with their minds. And the same with food. They could help their crops grow, but they still used the land. There were those that could, as you would think, create something out of thin air, but a lot of energy was put into that. So other methods were used, crystals especially.

How were they used?

Again with the power of the mind, by linking with a crystal they would find its special purpose and adapt to the world around them rather than trying to get the world to adapt to their will. This is how they had progressed up until the shift, by understanding this.

So prior to the shift they were living in harmony with the earth and with nature?

Very much so. They loved beauty. Their culture was the arts. Their colors were so vivid.

They clearly lived in permanent settlements, but did they have cities as we would think of them now?

Yes. Many came together with the idea that they would learn. Their schools taught them how to harness the power of their thoughts, and those highest in the field of technology went out trying to find different ways to apply it. But as more people came together the more they also realized how they could use the power of each others' minds. There was a new surge of energy coming through from the earth, and as energy doesn't have a consciousness itself people could use it for whatever they wanted, including for their own ends.

With their minds they could send others mad. There was physical violence. But the worst were those who understood and were adept at what they could do, and who harnessed their energies together like a battery. They got into other people's minds, and would use their energy too. This was a complete mutation of their abilities, and not what was meant at all. It wasn't right, it wasn't the way that minds should work, but once made it was hard to break their contact with others' minds.

Was this all as a result of them having free will?

Yes they had free will, but they also didn't have a soul plan as you do now. Their life purpose was left up to them to decide during their incarnation. This was also changed after this time. We learned that within an incarnate body it is very hard even for a very evolved soul to truly remember about spirit and so on if beforehand they don't have a plan set in place to do so. There is a baseness associated with the earth, and that baseness can draw souls who are power-crazed.

All around the globe we have ancient traditions and sacred texts that talk about a 'Golden Age' and how it collapsed into decadence. Presumably this is what you are describing for us now?

Yes. Hedonism, power struggles and violence ensued. It was meant that signs would be left, that could be rediscovered at a time when this could happen again. This is the imprint, it is a memory imprinted on all our souls of what not to do.

What happened to end this previous civilization, was there some sort of upheaval?

I was part of the council back then. We discussed with those that oversee the earth how best to stop this. The earth was aware that it had its own power whereby it could grant great fertility, but it could also wreak much havoc. A contract was struck. Myself and others did not want to know exactly what would happen as we had chosen to incarnate at that time, to help to take many souls away into the light as it ended.

So many of us were needed to make sure that those who needed to move on were moved away from the edge of the energy as the ripple effect moved out into the surrounding spaces. We knew something would happen naturally. Where I was a wall of water as high as a mountain hit us. Then many of us hovered above the scene as we watched what happened below, before we took those souls we needed to with us. And the earth shook and shook, and eventually the water took what it needed to and cleansed it. Everything came from water first, so everything went back. It was right of the earth to do it this way.

So it was an earth thing, not the impact of a comet or anything like that?

Not *that* time.

Perhaps I can ask you about yourself. Are you one of the entities we talked to last time?

No. I have been brought in to speak at this time because I was present during the last shift. It was the last time I incarnated on earth.

You mentioned that you were on the 'council' back then too, perhaps you can tell us a little more about that?

There were many of us from different parts of the universe. We tried to combine our ideas, things that had worked in other places. But duality on the earth is within everything that lives on it, so those things that had worked in other places didn't necessarily work here. People were drawn too much to extremes to appreciate them. You could say I was the centre of the council. I had also come from somewhere else, but I understood earth.

I was all for the project, and I was one of those who brought in these souls from elsewhere with their own experiences. I expected the level of soul advancement on earth to be such that they would succeed. There were many of us, so it wasn't just my decision, but I shouldered the responsibility with the others when it did not go according to plan. And afterwards I pledged to help the next time around.

What proportion of the human population was wiped out by this upheaval?

Only about forty percent. Those that remained were in places where the land was not so fertile, but also the energy was not so strong and they had not been so corrupted.

What size of population did the earth have then?

Not even one percent of what we have now.

Is this former civilization what some people would refer to as 'Atlantis'?

It is. Not that we called it that, but the word itself

has a resonance that energetically awakens those who were involved at the time to a memory, an imprint. We hope this means that when they feel the new energy now it will not be corrupted again. It is an important word.

Because of its resonance?

When people say it they are filled with hope and optimism.

New beginnings?

Yes.

Have a lot of the souls that were there during the last shift returned to experience this one?

Yes. Although most have been having experiences in other places in the meantime, many of them were horrified with what they had done, and have been determined to make sure that if they experienced it again they would not be corrupted.

You see these people more in certain parts of the world. There are those in the East who are already able to manipulate energy to change certain things. You may have read about them, for example monks in the Himalayas, and Tibet in particular, which resonates completely with Atlantis. And souls that had very fluid form last time have tended to select these types of lives now, for this change, so they can again be partly removed from society and go back into those memories of how to change and shift energy.

You suggested in the last session that the outcome was known last time round, whereas this time it's not. Can you explain how that works given what you've just told us?

Those above me, for want of a better word, did know that this experiment of bringing in energy to a place of duality, and trying things that had worked in other places, would not work. They knew that we had much to learn about the soul, and how much it could remember while still functioning within the human form. But we needed to learn this. Perhaps that's why this is still so painful to me, because I believed so truly that it would work. But you're right, they did know that this experiment wouldn't work, at that level it was always known. Yet we learned so much from it that, even though I and others felt it was a failure at the time, subsequently there was a massive leap in evolution as a result of what was learned.

Is it not the case that nothing is ever a failure because it is all experience?

It was a failure in my eyes because of the part I played, but overall it wasn't. The earth itself discovered that it could focus its attention as well. Up until that point it had never been asked to focus its attention within itself to actually change the forces around it and make something happen in a specific place. So it too was discovering about itself.

Can we return to the issue of when this last upheaval happened?

26,000 years ago. The earth used the surge of energy to be able to do these things.

There appears to be physical evidence on the earth that there was a major comet impact about 11,500 years ago, which would have decimated the global population. Is that something you could confirm?

It wasn't something I was involved in.

Perhaps we could ask whoever can answer that question to step forward?

[This new energy later identified themselves as a

'helper of Source'. Janet noted subsequently that it felt somewhat remote and aloof.]

There was involvement across the universe, and the earth was impacted just like a number of other places. This was going to happen and therefore the earth used it as a time of purification. The weather systems would change so that it would be encased. So while there was an encasement on the outside, much energy could be stored and nourished within. It knew it was preparing for a time when there would be many things living on its back. So it was a way to prepare for such a time. It was basically taking advantage of an event that was going to happen, and affect other parts of the universe, anyway.

Do you mean that it absorbed the energy of the impact itself and was able to store it in some way?

The energy was taken inside, and the casing on the outside gave it time to infuse this energy into every particle on the earth before it could be lost to the atmosphere. There is always much energy stored within the earth that is let out as and when it's needed.

So the earth itself had a major cleansing 26,000

*years ago, and then there was another major
episode as a result of the comet impact 11,500
years ago?*

The change 26,000 years ago actually made the
earth more fertile throughout, so although it
reduced the human population significantly it had
less impact on the earth itself. 11,500 years ago
was a dramatic change for the earth, preparing it
for the situation we're now in with so many souls
on its face.

*But presumably a significant proportion of the
human population was wiped out 11,500 years
ago as well?*

They were, but population had dwindled anyway
because we knew this was going to happen. Many
souls chose not to incarnate at that time and just
to watch, or they continued their journey in other
places. Not so many people were wiped out then
as is commonly thought because less people
were on the planet.

*Perhaps I can just ask you about yourself. Are you
on the council that looks after the earth?*

Shall we say I am an advisor to a number of
different places. It's best for me not to say exactly

where I am from at this time, except that I can answer this: I was part of the process that impacted the earth at that time. There was a wider picture involved, it was something that had to happen. I am a 'helper of source'. I do not have a name that you would understand.

the shifts before that

To go right back to the fundamentals, do universes get created one after the other, and does each one somehow become more refined?

More or less. Each one concentrates on different qualities, different things it has learned from the universe before. The universe we are in now is discovering the full range of the physical. No universe before has been so solid.

So there is a sense of building on and learning from what went before?

Absolutely. The consciousness remains. Some universes previously were not much different from each other, but this one is very different.

To return to the 26,000 year cycle, has this had an impact on life on earth from the outset?

Since the earth came into existence it has had an impact, because since that time there have been the beginnings of living organisms. Anything that lives on the earth goes through the earth's shifts and changes with it, so these are displayed or at least mirrored in each organism's energy field.

It goes right back to the beginning and the sea.

The seas and the oceans were always the breeding grounds, the experimental laboratories. It took many, many years for the right types of organisms to start coming through that could have a consciousness within them.

Was this being directed in any way?

You would call it the 'hand of God'. There had to be a lot of direction from other places, lots and lots of different places that already had lifeforms came together to create something new, something different. It took longer than was expected as this was always going to be a place of duality, and that hadn't been experienced before. For things to be set up properly it all had to be perfect, the perfect surroundings, otherwise it was all just going to die out again, and nobody wanted that. So there was a lot of direction initially, before we could sit back and see what would happen once soul consciousness took over and did what it wanted with those bodies.

The earliest human forms appeared a couple of million years ago. Were there any problems with sophisticated soul energy trying to work with bodies and brains that weren't particularly advanced?

No, because the soul energies coming in were relatively inexperienced and not very aware of their own potential at that time. Everything went at its own pace while physical form evolved and became more sophisticated. The very earliest consciousnesses that went into human form were brand new. They needed what you would now consider to be very, very simple lives. Emotions hadn't been brought in, and many other attributes that you would now consider to be associated with a human soul were not there. The first thing they had to master was survival. Without learning about a need to survive, progression could not have happened, and this had to be achieved before they could bring anything else in. You would not recognize their energy as a human energy now.

How long have what we would refer to as 'modern humans' been on the planet?

It's hard to answer as the level of consciousness and the level of energy body are different things, and we have experimented with many different combinations over the course of human history. You have been as you are now for approximately 5000 years.

Ok, to put it another way, when did reasonably advanced soul forms first start to be able to incarnate on planet earth in some sort of a human-like body?

75,000 years ago.

Does that mean there was a major step forwards at this time in terms of the sophistication of the soul energy and the physical body?

That's the time that, if you encountered that soul energy now, you would understand it as human. Earlier than that you would not.

Is the date of 75,000 years meant to represent three cycles ago?

Yes.

On a more general note, have highly evolved souls incarnated at various times in human history to assist the development of human culture?

It's happening the whole time. Humans come into the world with amnesia, so from a very early age they rely on and look to others for knowledge. So self-discovery and growth needs to be encouraged by those who are more 'evolved' as you would say, or as we see it those whose purpose is for the whole not the one. They choose to remember more, to instinctively 'know' from soul, and feel compelled to share this with others.

Many religious icons throughout the world have been on this path, in fact all the main ones in every religion. Each shared their knowledge at appropriate times to introduce great change, and the energy of these learnings is what remains. And religion is only one vehicle. Progression is inevitable, and wisdom is not exclusive to religion, the opposite in fact. You'll find it in the inspirational souls who have been leading lights in, for example, science, literature, art, music, health and politics – those who have tapped into a part of themselves that connects us with everything, and then used it to bring new and inspired knowledge through. You can see it now in popular culture, in those who have overcome adversity, illness or disability and then shared their inspired learnings with others.

Highly evolved souls often incarnate in the unlikeliest of bodies, in which they are not seen as glamorous or alluring by the masses. They work alone or in small groups to change the course of history, introducing progressive change in difficult times. This has always been the way, from the time when souls first chose amnesia.

Presumably by 'amnesia' you mean that once incarnate we don't consciously remember that we are soul energies whose real home is in the light realms. But when did souls first choose to have this amnesia?

Towards the end of the Golden Age, shortly before the last shift, humans were progressing well. The bodies of those who are your ancestors today had evolved fully into the now recognizable human form, and life was thriving. Initially amnesia was just an experiment, not all chose it. Those who felt they would learn more with amnesia were the pioneers, but their fate was to be an unknown without their memories from before. They would either succeed in integrating and learning from society, or they would become outcasts due to their 'baseness'.

When souls returned home they found they had learned much from this, especially the difficult experiences, so it wasn't long before all souls chose this route. But then many of them started to take the wrong path, and instead of creating they became destructive.

Ah, so it was the amnesia experiment that

caused the havoc just before the last shift. What happened before souls had amnesia?

Before this, when souls incarnated in human form they brought with them the group memories of the human race, much as most animals still do now. This was the only way they could survive and still evolve.

So what happened after the last shift, when the amnesia experiment went wrong?

Souls continued to reincarnate with amnesia, but we had to change the rules, so we introduced the idea of individual life plans and triggers to help people remember what they were supposed to be doing. And that was much more of a success, indeed it is how you still operate today.

Did anything important happen during previous energy shifts in the 26,000 year cycle?

Around 75,000 years ago there was a major upheaval that caused a bottleneck in human evolution [this must be a reference to the well documented Toba super-eruption]. So souls from elsewhere decided to use that energy shift to introduce some major changes. They chose one strain of surviving human, and they continued to influence the evolution of their physical bodies to improve their chances of survival, although by influence we mean energetically and not by physical, genetic experiments as some of you seem to believe. From that point on all the other strains, including the Neanderthals, started to die out, even if it took some time for them to become completely extinct. It is no coincidence that the evidence of these extinct human forms has been unearthed in the last hundred and fifty years, in order that in the run up to the current shift we would be able to reveal what was really going on from a soul perspective.

In the next shift, around 50,000 years ago, there was no major upheaval. But because by then humans had properly mastered basic survival, the emphasis switched from influencing physical development to influencing emotional development. Then culture could progress much faster and people could come together to live in larger, more settled communities. Also over time humans started to have longer life spans and more individualized soul memories, and this is what developed into the Golden Age before the last shift.

Do we always have help from souls from other

places during these shifts?

Yes, because the shift of 75,000 years ago was such a resounding success, and these souls can bring in ideas that have been tried in different environments. But progression happens within the cycles too, there are constant developments and evolution taking place. Then it's as if a new surge of energy comes through to feed the next 26,000 years. And so the cycle of growth, progression, experience and expansion continues.

So does this cycle represent an uplifting of earth's energy vibrations each time?

It's two steps forward, one step back. It's always increasing, but it gets very depleted in that time, so the surge has to take into account what's been depleted and then add more besides.

So the current shift is just another part of this cycle, but it's becoming progressively more sophisticated and the energy levels are going up all the time?

They are. The difference is also in the number of consciousnesses present, not just human but animal. And you have very many spiritual consciousnesses without physical form that inhabit the earth too. This hasn't been done before, which is why this shift is quite different.

So what causes the 26,000 year cycle?

The universe is set up in such a way that variations within it will prevent it from becoming stagnant, there will always be scope for change to varying degrees. The universe is a masterpiece of design, architecturally complex even when viewed from the perspective of the dimension you reside in. Through science and mathematics you've discovered some of the rudimentary forces governing your solar system, and indeed the universe, and you begin to understand its nature. It is architecturally perfect for its purpose, which is to constantly change and evolve. The constant and infinite alignments being made throughout direct energy, which then propels and activates change, so everything is constantly moving forward.

Of these infinite alignments the one that affects the earth every 26,000 years has a specific purpose. It was set up to influence more than just your planet, but due to its magnetic nature the earth isn't just part of the alignment, it's central to it. Its movement to a slightly different position ensures it is in direct alignment to receive energy from many other parts of the universe, and indeed dimensions too. And it is magnetically weak enough that it has a greater capacity for change to take place.

You'll find reference to this cycle in the calendars, astronomical predictions and sacred geometry of your historical civilizations, to guide the way for future generations and to give them something to aspire to.

The wobble of the earth's polar axis, which we refer to as 'precession', has a 25,920 year cycle. Does that have anything to do with all this?

Yes. Nothing on this scale happens by chance, and this apparent 'imperfection' was deliberately created and designed so that earth's alignments with other parts of the universe would constantly change. This technique is used elsewhere too.

souls moving on to other places

Can you explain about parallel universes? Is this something we will experience as a result of this change?

That's where some people will leap. There is another place just like this. You won't find it as you look out of your telescopes towards the universe, it's set up in another place in another time. And those that find the correct route will find it.

Is there only one 'other place'?

There's the question. The answer's infinite. As the raising of the vibration happens you'll see what you want to see. It's a similar experience to what you call death. Your reality afterwards is what you want it to be. All the realities are out there, it's what you decide to see, and you'll be taken there.

Much has been said about the actual dates in December 2012. What relevance do these dates have for this energetic shift?

It's about the celestial connection. The alignments. Everything in place. Think of it as a super highway. If many souls are going to go to different places that they haven't been before, they have to have a vehicle to help them there. It doesn't mean this is a set time and place because things change day by day. But this is a date to work towards, and for souls to start to awaken consciously to the awareness of what might be happening, so they follow the path when they get there.

Can you explain that a little more clearly in the sense of what these people might actually experience?

It's like following a path, an energy path beneath your feet on the earth, like ley lines, but these are paths set up in the heavens. Not everyone will be doing this, but there are certain pockets of souls that will be going to other places, and they'll feel a pulling from their heart to these places. So it's the same thing, it's like following the energy beneath your feet, but this is high above, and so it's a helping hand, a guide to take them to the relevant place.

So much of the universe has to be involved because we couldn't do this without the help of energies from the other places they're going to. The leap will actually shift them into a different place. And they're not just leaving the earth, they're leaving what you call 'home' too. And so many going together will see a leap that has not been seen for so long. It should be a time of rejoicing. The earth is growing, as are all the souls on it.

So does that mean their physical body will die at this time?

Well their energy will go, so yes.

Do we have a percentage of the population that has chosen to do this?

It's a minority.

So is all this almost a bit of an experiment for you too?

Completely. This is why so many souls have wanted to come from other places. There is no fear when they come though, everyone knows their soul survives, and they take their chances.

SESSION 2

[At this point in the second session, having established that we needed to talk to a different energy about this topic, the new energy revealed that they were the first of the two we spoke to in the first session.]

Last time you mentioned souls using the energy shift to propel them to other places. Can you tell us more about that?

There are a number of other places that are similar but not the same as the experience on earth. Places where souls experience emotions, for example. Many of those places have been set up alongside earth for eons, such as Sirius, and now they have opened the door to many more souls coming in, and this is an ideal time to do this.

There are also other places that are in other dimensions, and this is another shift, you might even refer to it as in a different time as well as a different space. If you could see all this it would look like a grid, it's almost like setting coordinates, just as now if you were planning a journey on earth you would use coordinates. The knowledge will be within to help people. It's another way of souls having their coordinates set to a new destination so that they can get there quickly.

What kind of bodies exist in other places that are physical? Is there anything like human form elsewhere?

In some places the bodies are very similar indeed.

In others it's more as if the consciousness exists without a body. Individuality still stands strongly, and there are experiences to be learned from in these places, but a physical body is not needed.

Do these latter experiences occur in physical or nonphysical environments?

All possibilities exist.

What proportion of the souls going on to other places have spent most of their incarnations on earth, rather than coming from other places?

It was agreed that this 26,000 year cycle would be a good time for change, as many councils had met due to earth souls requesting other experiences. Many had now experienced most of the things they could or wanted to on earth. So this was a good time to utilize the shift to take them to other places, and the majority that are doing this are those who have had predominantly human experiences to this point.

In the last session you mentioned that only a minority of the human population would be going off to these other places, but can you now give us a percentage?

Fifteen to twenty percent perhaps. It's a minority,

but with the amount of people on earth at this time it's still a very large number, which hasn't happened before. You will have witnessed this already. Never before have so many people led such extreme lives. Never before has there been such a need for therapists such as yourselves. When many souls who had not considered such a change before heard this was happening they decided to speed up the rest of their earth experiences, perhaps taking on three or four times what they might have worked through in previous incarnations, because they too wanted to go on this journey.

Some are going as soul groups as well. And because there will always be some that are more advanced in the group than others, they are helping each other to make the changes they need to. So there is much activity on the earth at this time, which can make it quite uncomfortable for those who aren't going through that experience.

So the increase in therapy and so on is all to help people to work through far more than they normally would?

Very much so. Many expressed a wish to

complete their unresolved issues prior to the energetic shift so they would be able to appreciate and accept it fully. The help given speeds up this process.

Can you explain how incarnating on earth helps souls to go to other places?

While you are incarnate you can experience extremes that you cannot experience without a physical form. While you are immersed in love in your spiritual home you do not push yourself to extremes. The survival instinct that is within all of you when incarnate, and is your most base quality, drives these extremes. But when you are at an extreme level, a new surge of energy coming through can create new possibilities. That is why this can be used as a vehicle to attain these other places, whereas souls immersed in love might not be at the frequency level that is most appropriate to take in this energy to make the leap. It's not necessary but it is a help.

And unlike the negative 'battery effect' that arose during the last shift, this time it will be used in a positive way by many, many souls, so that those who are struggling will be taken along by the others, and those who are stronger will take the weak with them. It will be a time when souls merge, but in the correct way, without corruption.

And this merging will take place only when they are no longer in physical form?

Yes, and only for a short time.

So this isn't the only way to attain these other places?

They could do it while in nonphysical form, indeed some are doing just that. But they are missing out on an experience that only comes round once every 26,000 years. So many have simply chosen to do this because it's an adrenalin rush, as you would call it, like nothing else.

Are these other places also going through shifts in their own right?

Most are stable now. A few aren't fully stable, but only those souls who are prepared for the next stage to be an unknown quantity will be going to them. Most will be going to places where there will be stability and a rest really. A rest for their energy while it stabilizes and gets used to these new places. And they will be changing frequency too.

And most of these souls have never experienced places like these before?

That's correct.

Do these souls all have contracts to go to specific other places, is that already decided?

Most have decided within their groups, and will travel in their groups. These may not be their primary groups, but they are the ones they are in for this shift.

How many of these other places are there?

If you could see the grid it would look like a maze. There are so many different places, but the choices are limited because there might be a similar experience to be had in any number of them. Overseers will have decided where the most appropriate place is for each soul. Some are choosing a break, and others are choosing a more challenging role.

You said just now that souls can experience emotions in some of these other places, so does that mean they have full duality like the earth?

None have the duality that earth has, they tend to be more gentle emotional environments. For many it will be a familiar thing to still have emotions, this will help them through this time of change. But they will only be emotions that we would describe as comfortable and happy.

So earth really is unique in terms of its duality?

In this part of the universe, in this dimension, yes.

Can you explain? Do you mean there are other physical parts of the universe that have environments similar to that of earth?

The universe is immense, and there are those that oversee different parts. There are other councils, and if it is happening here there is no doubt it will be happening in other parts as well. But in terms of the part we deal with there is only a place for one such environment with duality.

What about the dimension issue?

It's to do with vibration and frequency. There are other dimensions where everything has a slightly different vibration and frequency, so they would look and feel much the same as the one you're in now, but be slightly different. A slight change can change the perception and experience of a place significantly, and again there are councils that are in tune with that.

Does that mean there are other places very much like earth, just on a different vibrational frequency?

Yes.

Some people think there are an infinite number of replicas of the physical earth, where the experience is only minutely different between each one. Can you comment on whether or not that is correct?

It is to a degree. There are other places within the universe that are playing out similar stories as it were, and if there is a benefit to your soul experience you can go to these other places without taking your physical form. There is a way to step between these dimensions at the same time, and some people know how to do this while still incarnate.

To clarify, some people suggest that if I move my left little finger a little bit, for example, that creates one reality, and then there is another one created at the same time in which it is my right little finger that moves. Do new parallel realities get created every time even the slightest decision is made?

That's not the way we perceive it. It's not as straightforward as that. It's more about the thought processes that are going on, and the group reality that is being created.

So as souls we come together to create group experiences, we don't do it individually?

It is as a group, that's correct.

You mentioned Sirius as one of the other places, is that a physical experience?

Yes.

Does it have human-type life forms on it?

It would feel familiar for a human soul to be in that body, and many of the souls going there have had experiences there already, before coming to earth. So even though they have led the majority of their lives on earth, many have happy memories of Sirius and they will gladly return there. Souls who want a more peaceful next incarnation are going there.

Are there any other planets in our solar system that play host to soul experience, even if it's not as part of a physical existence?

There has been an investigation of possibilities on

each and every one of the planets in our solar system. This is why we are drawn to explore those planets. It's why some souls still believe we could exist on some of those planets. Unfortunately for them the memory is still very strong of a time when we possibly could have generated some sort of life form on those planets. None would support life as they are now, but there is a memory. The solar system is like a family, these are all siblings and there is a connection between them.

So there was a time when the other planets in the solar system could have supported life?

Not life as you perceive it, but there were consciousnesses that worked within each to see if some form of life that could hold consciousness could be created on them.

Did that ever happen on any of them?

There is a substance like water on Mars, and there have been similar experiments there to the one when we first started experimenting with the earliest life forms in the water on earth.

But there wasn't advanced life on Mars a long time before earth?

No.

Apart from Sirius are there any other stars that we would recognize where souls will be going during the shift?

You have telescopes now that can see the birth of stars, and some souls will be moving on to help with developing these new star systems. It's a slightly different consciousness, they will be using their experience of creation from the previous civilization, and of being part of what you might consider a blending of soul consciousness, to achieve this. But although they will connect with other souls there will still be strong individuality, so only those souls that have a strong sense of self have been allowed to take on such a mission. And we call it a mission because it is such.

At the birth of a new star system it is incredibly important that consciousness goes in to oversee the new creation within it, and only those who will stay true to the mission and not introduce their own agenda are selected. But these places can be seen on your telescopes, they're not that far away.

In the last session you mentioned a 'super highway'...

We prefer the term 'grid'.

Ok, you said that souls will be using this grid to attain other places via some sort of celestial alignment in 2012. But you also said there is no definitive date for this shift because it changes from day to day. How can both of these things be true?

This grid is immense and goes in many different directions, and as the celestial alignments change the access to these other places on the grid opens up. So the date that is talked of is like a lynchpin in all of this, but it is not the only one, it is just one alignment and one that can be seen with your telescopes. There is a lesser one in November 2011 that will be noticeable, then the main ones will be approximately a year apart. It will be as if there is a crescendo, with different things happening at different times, but roughly a year apart up to 2015.

So about five major alignments?

There could be as many as seven, depending on what happens. Seven is the number of completion. As always things may need to be adapted.

And everything will be completed by 2015?

In respect of souls who are moving on, yes, but the full changes and adaptation on earth will take longer. In 2015 the energy in the grid will be reversed back into the earth to help those that are struggling with the adjustment and the frequency change, so they may feel a resurgence that is simply this energy coming back into the earth.

When each alignment occurs, is it a physical alignment to the places they are going to?

It's more that you would look at the gaps where they have a clear path without the pull of other planets and stars in the way, ones that you might not be able to detect. Electromagnetism comes into play here, this is a way for them to go without being pulled to places they shouldn't go to.

So the alignments are all about getting the gaps right?

Exactly.

Will there be other souls acting as guides to help these souls as they journey across the grid?

Yes, there are many waiting. Many have come

from the places they are traveling to. Many are even waiting as we speak, and have chosen not to take on anything else until this time has passed. There will always be some souls who will leave before their due date as well, so guides will be waiting for them to make sure they go to the correct places.

So if there are only between five and seven major alignments, does that mean there are only this number of places souls are going to?

The alignment simply means there is space for them to go, but each time they will be going out in many directions to many different places.

On a similar tack, if there are between five and seven major alignments, does that mean we are looking for the same number of physical events in which their lives will be taken?

It is likely that these will be times when the majority of the souls involved will leave in what you would describe as natural upheavals.

Are these going to be spread all around the globe?

Yes, there will be nowhere that is untouched by this.

We have had some major upheavals already, for example the tsunami in Indonesia. Was that the beginning of this process?

That was more in the way of preparation. Many of those souls are already incarnate again now but in a new, more evolved, energy body. And there are children who will come of age as the shifts happen who will be comfortable with the new energies, and they will become the new leaders, although this will be more in an advisory than in a leadership role as we know it at present. They will find that people gravitate to them to make it more comfortable for themselves. They may be leader advisors within communities or within whole countries.

So the major upheavals so far have not been of the same type as the ones to come?

They are necessary in that the earth is like a huge muscle flexing itself, getting ready for what it needs to do, and as this happens there will naturally be what you would call upheavals. And because the earth is so populated there is nowhere this can happen without many souls being a part of it, so they have already agreed to this. They are not so much going to other places though, it's just that this was their time and they had agreed to help the earth.

In terms of future upheavals, are there any major ones planned for this year, 2010?

There will be three more this year related to preparation for the energetic shift.

Is this also the start of souls going to other places?

The vibrational energy is changing, but it's only just starting to change noticeably in people's physical bodies, so not many people are choosing to leave for other places yet as part of their original plan. Some are getting ready to help others in the next series of events. They are more at what you would call guide level.

Will all the people who get caught up in the upheavals from 2011 onwards be going to other places?

No. There will be many where it is just their time to leave this incarnation as normal. But more generally the reason this process works both for the earth and for the souls involved, though it may sound distasteful while still in a human body, is that the adrenalin and fear felt just before the event will help to propel their energy as a group, and remind them all to go as one. It's not that suffering is needed, but this extreme emotion at the point of death in a large group of people will be needed, or at least appropriate, for the major leaps to other places.

Please remember also that this has been agreed, they know what is going to happen and they know that any suffering will be momentary, relatively speaking. As soon as they leave their bodies it will be different, they will feel that pull, they will feel the coordinates kick in. They will not have the same choices as normal, that is to stay and think and ponder what's just happened. It will be too quick. By the time they think of that they will be halfway to their destination.

We hear many people talking about a 'pole shift'. Is this likely?

That is happening, it's one of the things the earth is processing. The weakening of the magnetic field will actually help the souls going to other places.

Does this mean big climate changes?

Relatively speaking the magnetic field does not

affect climate as much as it may affect many species of animal, particularly those living in the sea. It will be confusing because their coordinates will not work any more. But it is a time of evolution for them as well, and the strongest will survive.

In the last session you mentioned that some of the people going to other places are shifting their 'home' too. Can you clarify this?

The home we are referring to is the place that soul consciousness goes to between lives. It's a place where you have no physical body and your frequency is different. It's also where you can connect with your higher self to enable all your soul memories to come through, and where you can be an active part of Source as a whole. But each dimension shall we say has its own home. Some other places are in a different dimension or vibration, so their home is different too, even though it will still feel familiar.

Would it be best to think of these different 'homes' just as different vibrational aspects of the one home rather than as different 'places'?

Yes.

Is there anything else you think we need to know

about souls moving on to other places?

Only that the actual experience of leaving will feel like a 'pulling'. A very quick, rapid pulling that comes from the heart centre. This is how we've decided to do it this time, to take the mind out of the equation. We don't want to take free will away, but we also expect that there would be a lot for these souls to contend with if they had the normal thought processes immediately after death.

We have an assumption that a soul will experience pretty much what it expects to after death, at least initially. Is this normally correct?

Yes. Normally what they experience is their own reality, although it is influenced by their guides helping them to project whatever they want. But in the current special circumstances there will be guides around who will be helping with the energy coming from the heart, and almost shielding the mind from any confusion until a later time when they can safely go through that. So the experience isn't being taken away, it's just being saved til a slightly later time.

All of this is clearly going to result in a significant reduction in global population levels. Can you give us an idea of the most likely percentage reduction?

Approximately twenty-five percent.

But presumably there is some flexibility around that because of free will?

It could be as much as forty percent if violence breaks out again. We can estimate approximately how many people will ignore and block the change, those who will find it more and more difficult and resort to violence. But we have estimated it as quite a low number, and perhaps that reflects our optimism that this time humans will tune into their souls more. However if more struggle and resist and there is more violence, that may taint those who have opened up and they may revert back as their survival instinct kicks in. Remember this was the first instinct instilled, and under pressure it will always override all others.

We haven't really discussed what we refer to as 'global warming', but one of the things predicted is that large parts of the globe will suffer severe water shortages. Is that your understanding too?

Once the shift has occurred and the population

has been reduced, the earth has a great capacity to heal itself quickly, and therefore a water shortage is unlikely.

Is there anything else about the reduction in global population levels that you think we should know at this time?

Only that generations have been working on this for some time. It's not something they have suddenly thought about and are hurriedly trying to achieve. Many have been working on this from even thousands of years ago. Those who are interested in planning their destiny will have mapped out many incarnations to reach this point, often along with the rest of their soul group.

Normally how someone progresses in an individual life will change what they want to do next. But those that plan far ahead are usually pretty much past their own main growth on earth. They still have their own soul experiences, but they are more in control of those experiences, and are finishing off, and are there more for others.

life on a more highly evolved earth

For those who remain here on earth, what will their experience be like?

Even we can't say. It's a new experience with this evolved body. We can estimate how many will awaken comfortably, and those who will fight it, and those who will put themselves in harm's way. Those who will be able to cope with it and those who can't. But we're watching with as much interest as you.

What actions should people take to change their vibration?

It will naturally happen as the vibration changes for those who choose to see not with their eyes.

Is there some way they can learn how to do that?

Humans never did quite learn. They always try too hard. Be like the animals, just let it happen. They know what's going on, they don't question.

Is there a way that an individual can influence what happens to them during this change?

Don't fight against the tide. You've already put everything into sequence in your life plan. All that's taking over is your consciousness of what you *think* you want to happen. Your soul already knows what's going to happen, so just let it happen. The key to everything is finding comfort and joy in change. Not to fight against it will be the most comfortable route, the path of nonresistance. Those who do resist will struggle, they'll be the ones who suffer, but it's not true suffering because they're just working on another experience.

As we move forward what's the most likely outcome for the global economy? Will human beings still need money?

Yes. Trade is always needed. No one person can provide everything for themselves. So trade is necessary, and money is a good vehicle for this. However the economy as we see it now will 'crash and burn' as you say. The international, global economy will collapse, and trade will be more local, so the same levels of bureaucracy will not be needed.

Is that definite?

It's not a definite, but it's the most likely outcome if the shifts and changes happen as we expect them to. There will be a lot less people living on the planet. The way people live will be so different, international exchange will not be necessary. It will shift and change and bend to what humans need, as has always been the case.

How will communities best organize themselves in the future?

People will naturally gravitate to others that they resonate with, and through that they will come up with their own plan as to the appropriate way to live. Some of the ways to live will be very similar to now. Others will find they understand more about themselves if they're closer to nature, and they will separate themselves off to do this.

Will there be any form of international travel?

Nothing is ruled out, nothing will completely stop. But the desire will be different. Desire drives humans in everything they do, so if the desire goes it will naturally recede. But nothing is impossible.

Are we planning to move away from duality here on earth?

There will always be a place for duality. The earth itself is set up in a way that life can only exist with some form of duality. But there will be more middle ground.

Less of the extremes?

Extremes were needed as a vehicle to take us to this place we're at now, but once the changes occur they won't be required.

SESSION 2

[At this point in the second session, having established that we needed to talk to a different energy about this topic, the new energy revealed that they were the second of the two we spoke to in the first session.]

Can you tell us anything more about what life will be like for those who continue to live on a more highly evolved earth?

As a whole it will be a wonderful time of great change. Yet it will only feel wonderful for those who can really embrace change and live in the present. There will be a period of serious disruption too, so it's inevitable that many people will find it very hard not to keep looking to the future and wondering what's going to happen next, and how they are going to cope. But those who can actually live in the present and enjoy these changes will progress in leaps and bounds.

Can we expect changes in people's thoughts and

behavior and so on?

People will still believe what they believed before. But in terms of religion, for example, it will be as if they have discovered something new within that religion that they hadn't noticed before, which will allow them to accept what is happening more. This is something new and exciting, but it's only an add-on. Rather than throwing away the past they will be tuning into existing things they had not noticed or resonated with before, once they have greater understanding.

Can you comment again on whether we will be tending to live in smaller, more self-contained communities?

Yes, as things happen throughout the earth people will feel the need to move, they won't feel as safe as before. They will learn quickly that they need to listen to what's going on around them, and to their own intuition in terms of what is safe. So they will feel less compelled to live in places they are not comfortable with, and the changes will make it easier for them to move elsewhere.

For those who are not best suited to the city and to large towns things will become increasingly uncomfortable, as their minds start to expand with this new energy. Touching the minds of those around them when they don't resonate with them will be quite uncomfortable. So they will go to more remote areas, or at least make sure they join with others who are thinking similar thoughts.

An increasing number of cooperative spiritual communities are being planned even now. Will we see a lot more of these springing up?

There will be a need for these initially, there will be shortages of fuel and power, but it's simply a time of adaption, there will not be too much hardship. It will mean people need to go back to basics though, for a time. Then in the longer term there will be more what you might call eco-towns.

Will there be any particular parts of the world that will naturally attract those with lighter energies?

Places that aren't overly populated at the moment, simply because there will be more space and less need for struggle between the people there. There will be power struggles in places that are overpopulated already.

But no particular parts of the world that have been singled out as 'beacons of light' or anything like that?

Much has been said about these types of places, but the earth has pockets all over. Every place has its merits and its pros and cons, and if we were to point out any particular places there would be a convergence of people on them anyway. So people should merely feel where they are drawn to, even if it is on the other side of the world.

In the last session you said that those who resist the new energies will feel increasingly uncomfortable. Can you tell us more about that?

It will be similar to having a breakdown. They will be trying to hold on to what is familiar, particularly in terms of wealth and material things, and when these are either taken away or not bringing them as much comfort it will be a breakdown of sorts. A feeling of paranoia that other people are taking these from them. They simply will not have accepted that there could be any wealth other than the material, ignoring the wealth of the mind.

But they will still carry on existing in the new vibrations, they won't be wiped out by them?

It is their purpose to remain. Even though the

duality will not be as extreme it will still be there, the earth cannot exist with only, as you would say, 'the positive'. There has to be a balancing of souls, even though that sounds quite cruel. As one vibration moves up there has to be another that goes denser.

Does that mean that the people not flowing with the shift are not less experienced souls, they're just experienced souls playing a different role?

They are generally quite experienced, yes. They are playing out the last parts of their earth experience, indeed the most difficult challenges they have chosen to date. But we're talking about such a small minority that it's not really balancing throughout, it's nowhere near as big as the number who will enjoy the experience.

Can you give us an idea of the percentage?

Five to ten, if that. But it might feel like there's more just because they will tend to be more explosive in their feelings.

But getting to this point will take time?

Yes.

What is your best estimate of when the major

aspects of the energy shift will be complete?

By the year 2020 we will have seen the majority of change, and it should all be complete by about 2030.

We as individuals have been noticing the energies really shifting quickly of late, almost exponentially. Would that be right?

Yes. This is the best part for us watching, as more people actively notice and become aware of the energy rising. And as they share their experiences others wake up to it too. It is *so* exciting for us to see this rapid awakening taking place as planned.

On a separate note, because of the human tendency towards elitism and so on, I have a concern that people reading this may tend to hope they are one of those moving on to other places, rather than staying here on earth. Do you have any views on how that can be avoided, or do we just flow with it?

There will be a resonance for the right people, and it would be a good thing for them to start waking up to the possibility. Also, would it help if we told you that the souls on planet earth at the moment are the most evolved and ready they have ever been? People will enjoy reading that. This is one of the reasons why it was decided that an experiment could take place where the results were not already known. It is why the earth agreed for so many souls to incarnate, even though they could literally plunder it within an inch of its life.

We all hope, and even pray you might say, that you will all access at least tiny nuggets of your soul memories, and remember that you are having a full blown experience involving extremes of almost every emotion you've previously felt. And whether you are moving on from earth or staying, you are evolved to the extent that you can handle such change even while in an incarnate body. Even those who choose to stay and then live a life where they do not awaken to this energy are still incredibly experienced and evolved souls, relatively speaking.

So there aren't many new or inexperienced souls on earth at the moment?

A tiny number, a very tiny number. We did not want any new souls to be put off from having physical form by entering a life that was so extreme. There are a few, but that's only as a balance.

Is there anything else we need to know about life on a more evolved earth?

It will be a 'fuller' experience, that is the best way to describe it. It won't be so physical. People will spend more time in a type of meditation, just in terms of how they live their lives, which will enable them to interact with various types of energy to create a more complete experience.

So meditation is important?

It's something people will naturally do without even calling it meditation. Just focusing their mind on changing and shifting things will take it into a meditative state, which will actually be quite calming for the body. So there will be less diseases, less disorders of the body, it will be easier to keep their physical form in a healthy state. It will then be more likely that when people leave their bodies it will be at the time of their choosing, and this is more how it used to be before.

Rather than because of illness or ill-health you mean?

That will still play a part for some. But for most, when they have got to a point where they are ready, they will be able to choose to leave quite comfortably, while others around them will be more aware and will not hold them back.

Partly this will be because those left behind will be able to talk to their loved ones who have gone. Not quite as you would think, not full conversations, because that would just be confusing for all, and those who had departed would be tempted not to move on. But there will be an awareness and therefore a comfort. As a result people will be able to let go of the past more easily, and to live in the present. And once you can do that you can see the wonderful opportunities around you.

Presumably we will all still suffer from the ageing process, that won't go away?

It won't, but it will be somewhat slowed down. Someone who is older may look a lot younger than they do currently, because the physical form will be easier to look after and be better nourished physically and energetically. People will easily live to be one hundred and beyond.

Most of the people being born now have an

evolved energy body. If tests were carried out you would see that their energy is quite different, and this will all help. And it has been going on for some time. Many are teenagers now, some even into their twenties, and their energy will act as a guiding light for many others who are struggling with the process. We have always known as incarnate souls to look to the wise and the elderly, and that will still partly be the case, but many will be looking at those who are younger because they will have brought more wisdom with them.

Does this also mean the veil of amnesia is being lowered for new souls coming in?

It is more that with this higher vibration they are more in tune with their higher self, and closer to it. They will still have amnesia about their past, but when they need information it will be easier for them to tap into it, and for it to come to them during meditation and sleep. And the more this happens the more it will be accepted, and they will not be seen as different or sick.

Is there anything else about them we would notice?

People will feel very comfortable around them. Those that don't are those on a slightly different

path who will naturally gravitate elsewhere. But
those going with the flow will naturally attune their
energies to them, and this will be an easier
process as their own energy opens up.

*Will this be true of the majority of children born
on earth from now on?*

The majority, yes.

*Does this mean both their physical body and their
soul energy are more advanced?*

There are some children even now who do not
get sick any more, and that is because their
physical body is more in tune with their energy
body.

*Presumably souls incarnating on earth in the
future will still be on their soul journey, but it will
just be a different kind of experience?*

Yes. It's another variation and a fuller experience.
Whereas before people may have been working
on emotions, that won't be so important any
more as their emotions won't be so extreme.

What sort of things will they be working on then?

They'll still be working on such things as
relationships to the earth as well as to others, but

it will also be about developing the new skill of expanding their energy out. This has been done before on a smaller scale, there have been many tribes where this was part of their culture, but never on such a global scale.

Can you explain more about this idea of expanding energy out?

It will be an experimental time. People will notice that once again they are able to do things with their minds. If they can remove fear they will find they can almost play with this new skill, and they will find how much it can help them. They will be able to project their minds to other places, for example to check for safety, or just to come into contact with other people, or to see what weather is coming. Whatever their choice of life they will find this new skill can be used in any area.

Will we be developing our telepathic abilities?

Some people will have a touching of minds where they can understand each other. But it will be more of a calling to someone, you would be able to think of them and they will think of you at the same time. You will know that you need to meet, or talk. That will be a skill that most people will be able to master relatively quickly.

Are we seeing this already?

Yes, and that's what people need to learn. This isn't something brand new, it's always been a possibility for some, it's just that the new energy coming through will allow *all* humans to do this. And it will be done more safely this time. The physical body will be more evolved so there will be a stronger tie that connects them when out of it, and it will be easier for them to reconnect after such an experience.

Why will this ability be important?

There will no longer be a need to travel to connect with people or see things, it will all be done on a different wavelength. People will be able to leave their body and meet up with other people, or go to see what is happening, or what weather is coming in. In other words they will be relying on their own natural resources rather than on technology to do such things.

And they will be fully conscious while doing it?

They can be, but some will choose not to be.

Can you talk about whether we will be introducing new forms of energy generation?

More and more people will be using the focus of their minds, so there will be a new technology that will harness the power of mind. However the majority of the forms of power that will be used are already here, even though many are only in their infancy.

Is there anything else you would like to say about the future of politics or of the global economy?

Whether you have wealth or not will make no difference after the shift. That's not to say be carefree with your money, it just means live in the present. Money and trade will always have a place, so it's common sense to keep some, and to surround yourself with a survival kit in terms of a home and food and so on. But long-term financial investments, for example, will be a thing of the past.

You're now seeing a new approach in the leaders coming through, in the freshness of their thinking, and in the people they use to advise them. They will be listening with more than just their ears. At this time of massive global change it is imperative that these leaders are highly evolved, so that they hold firm to their purpose and mission throughout. There are many in place already, and you will feel who these people are if you look at and listen to them with your heart, then you will know the truth. But they are still in a human body, so do not look to them to be perfect or never make mistakes.

[The following information was provided later in the second session by the excitable 'nature spirit' energy mentioned in the introduction.]

Can you tell us more about what life will be like for those going 'back to nature'?

I like the countryside! I like the ones who will be living in the countryside, they will be learning so much from the earth and from nature spirits. They will utilize nature a lot more, but not as now. They won't just use up the resources, they will actively give back to them as well. They will be able to influence the crops and everything living on the land with their minds to help it to grow. Especially after the shift, when they will need to grow crops quicker, they will find themselves using the energy from their hands and their minds. And getting together in communities will just speed this up even more.

There are some groups experimenting with this even now. And as more and more communities learn to do it they will share their knowledge as well, it will be a time of greater knowledge sharing.

Will you personally be helping this process?

Yes, I'm one of the ones who will help those in the countryside to learn to use the elements around them. I come from the elemental kingdom. And as the elementals or nature spirits progress through the energy cycles as well, they will be more inclined to work with humans rather than stay away from them. Humans might not realize it but they will be harnessing their help whenever they grow a crop, or freshen water, and so forth.

Can you tell us how people can get more in touch with elementals to work with them?

They're on a slightly different frequency and you need to be in tune with it. It's fair to say that the majority of humans are not sufficiently in tune to be able to contact them at this time, but even to have an awareness that they are around is very helpful. And give them respect, they respond to respect.

So just asking respectfully for their help?

Yes, even if you can't see them. The more the

energy within people is raised and the frequency changes, the more they will be able to interact with some of these nature spirits, although different people tend to be more in tune with one type of elemental than another.

our ability to accelerate the process

What can we do to help the process?

Awaken others. You've chosen to awaken early, which is a hard path, which is why we help you so much along the way. But where you're in the minority now, very soon you won't be. More and more people every day are becoming more and more aware, and that is the main role you play, in helping this.

Helping people to accept the concept of their soul living on after death?

Fear of change is the biggest obstacle. And bringing the longevity of their soul to people's awareness will help the expansion of the mind, but cannot be done if there is fear in place.

What's the best medium for us to help more people to understand this?

Through your own increased vibration. This is not intellect we're talking about. People resonate with vibrations, and those who are willing and open to new understanding will resonate and find the right people. It's not what you say, it's not even what you teach, it's what you give out on a vibrational level they will pick up.

What is useful for us to be putting in place at this time?

Possibilities. Giving people opportunities to see what's before them and to decide if they choose to think of these things fully now, or just open their eyes a bit for later. Possibilities are the greatest vehicle for us all to learn and grow, and to choose and change our experience.

SESSION 2

[Although some of these messages are more personally directed they have been included because they have a far broader applicability than just to ourselves.]

Apart from flowing with things, and meditating, is there any other advice you can give us about how we can assist the energy shift in ourselves as individuals?

As we start opening up our minds and discovering new talents, instead of them becoming an energy block within our system that we don't understand, our awareness will enable us to see where we can go with these energies, how they can work for us. This is the opening up of the mind that we talked about previously. There are many exercises for all this out there already, but using the ones that are easiest and simplest to remember will best ensure that people carry them out.

Are there any in particular that you would like to share with us now?

Simply for people to discover their own way to tune into their inner self, to go within before going outwards, in whatever way they resonate with. So meditation, as you say, and other simple techniques to go inside. But everyone is so different, that is why they need to discover their own technique for this.

Apart from meditation is there anything else we can do to open ourselves up to messages from our higher self or spirit guides?

Sound is very important. Different sounds resonate with different people. Music in particular will resonate with particular energy sites within the body, and so people should try to find music that enables them to go inside themselves.

Can that be any kind of music?

Certainly, and it will vary at different times in our lives, and depending on what we're going through.

Also for many with very busy lives who are not set up to think too much about such things, mediums such as television, films, books and other sources will be enough to open them up, and remind them at the correct time that there may be other possibilities.

If we switch now to how we can help others to wake up to the shift, will the broader use of regression and other therapy also have a significant role?

Yes, it's another way that people can reconnect with their souls. Anything that helps them to do that will be on the increase.

But was it always foreseen that at this time there would be more people doing this kind of work?

We originally thought there would be a huge number of souls, helping each other to come through all this together. When we realized this was not happening quite as much as we expected, with more conflict between people, some souls agreed to switch into a slightly different role to do this work. For some this wasn't in their original plan but it was renegotiated because their purpose was all about the soul growth of others, so they knew their contracts might change along the way.

You said in the last session that it's not what we say or write so much as the vibrations we give off that will be most important. Have you anything to add to that?

What you say or write is important, but it's the energy behind it that really matters. Two people can be teaching the same thing, but if one has an underlying energy of optimism, and love not fear, that will be picked up. If another teaches the same thing without this energy they will be less effective at waking people up.

So writing books and giving lectures and so on is still important?

Very important. But so is the energy behind it, and what we are doing now is an important vehicle to release that positive energy. It is also why we as a council are involved at this time. We would not be giving these messages if they were only to be heard by a few people. As much as we are happy to do that, it is important for many people to hear this, especially people who are struggling and looking for something that resonates with them that they have not yet found.

So is there anything we need to be aware of in terms of making sure this message gets to as many people as need it?

There will be many unseen helpers. But also don't forget that this is not simply a book, your purposes are entwined with these messages and you will all be speaking to people about them, giving lectures and so on, so the book is only part of it. And other people will pick up on them and start talking about them too, creating a real energy and excitement behind them.

How important is this work compared, for example, to our therapy work?

Each has its role. Many people will sort themselves out and shift things without being drawn to a therapist, so entertaining books and talks and documentaries will also help them to wake up.

It has been suggested that, rather than concentrating specifically on helping others, if we concentrate on our own growth, openness and happiness, the rest will just come. Is that correct?

That will help you to help others *so much*. This is

still a time of people's own soul growth and enjoyment – remember this must be for enjoyment. So you should go to wherever you will be happiest, not where you think you will help the most people, because wherever you are you will attract those you need to help. The more you can be what some who are not so in tune may even perceive as selfish, the better. There will be work wherever you go, and the more you are in places where you want to be and are happy, the lighter your own vibration will be and the more people and souls and consciousnesses you will attract and help.

Remember it's not just those you can see, you are giving this help in lots of different ways. Even with those people you only momentarily come into contact with, if it is their time to release certain elements, whether energies of their own or spirit attachments or whatever, sometimes your higher vibration will allow them to do this. So do not think you are ever being selfish.

What about people helping to clear the earth's own energy field?

Although it is not really the right word, there are large areas that need to be cleared of intense 'negative' energies trapped in the earth, which can still affect people's energy systems. There are a number of people doing this.

[At this point in the session the excitable 'nature spirit' energy mentioned in the introduction was so keen to talk to us he spontaneously took over.]

Is there anything else we need to know about the ways we can accelerate this process, whether in ourselves or others?

Be who you were born to be! There are so many wonderful souls here now who are in tune with themselves, and with us too. So shine that light! If you could look at all the souls now, as they really are with their light shining out, it's like fireflies at night. It's brilliant to watch from a distance as you look down and see all the people opening up! It's just so exciting, there's so many more people who are awake than you think! You can see them, I watch them at night, their night time, and it's my job to see where they still have some denseness and blockages. But these are getting less and less. It's wonderful, I can go through whole swathes of people and know that they can release what they need to on their own from now on.

More and more people are awakening through

every medium, this whole global shift is wonderful because it speeds everything up. The things people are seeing on television – isn't television wonderful! – and films, they have so many experiences, and virtual experiences, they get to understand and remember what it's like not to have physical form. And it's so much easier for them to open up than it's ever been.

why everything is as it should be

What's the purpose of the negative media hype about 2012?

No experience is worthwhile if it's easy. The role of almost half the souls here is to bring conflict in, to obscure what people start to see. And the energy that is created in overcoming these obstacles, and in changing awareness, is what's helping the planet itself to evolve and grow.

The earth agreed to have so many souls incarnate on its back for this period as that's helping it to evolve too. Humanity's parasitic nature is helping the earth to break free of its bonds, to increase its own vibrational level. So the things you see as bad that people have done to the planet are purely them fulfilling a soul-to-earth contract. To help it grow and do what it needs to vibrate out, to start moving up and shifting its own vibration. So everything you can think of is just a beautiful play that has an end in sight, and every character has to play their part to reach that end.

Do events like Haiti help people to wake up to who they are?

When someone sees what can happen in an instant to another human being, not only do they have compassion but they think about their own life, they think how quickly change can happen. And that in itself brings about awareness, and starts to loosen their whole bond with what they felt was the permanent nature of the world around them. They start to understand that change can happen in an instant. But they're also opening up to the fact that change can be for good as well as bad.

SESSION 2

We talked in the last session about the massively increased population and its pollution acting like a parasite on the back of the planet, which will in fact help it to raise its vibrations. Can we discuss that a little more now?

Yes, everything that is being done to the earth at present that we see as bad, for example taking its resources, will ultimately just enable it to fight back with a survival instinct similar to our own. It's calling on energy that it hasn't needed for quite some time to bring that back. There are people trying to help it now, and it's not that their efforts are futile, but the whole raising of consciousness will, in its own right, give the earth what it needs. As more people become aware of the shift, without realizing it they are energetically helping the earth, they are putting their emotions and energy into it, which will help the process.

So the earth is behaving just as we are, in that we all have to face obstacles to raise our energy levels so that we properly resonate with the shift. Is that correct?

Yes. And the earth is calling in resources it hasn't needed for a long time. Mining is particularly important. Over the last few hundred years this has depleted so many resources deep within the earth that it needs to make drastic changes and literally push its energy outwards.

We have a concern that this might be misinterpreted by some as meaning they don't have to care about the pollution of the earth, but we suspect this is not what you intend at all. Can you clarify that for us?

What you are telling them are truths they learned before birth, and they will wake up to that. For those whose path is to pollute the earth, when they read these messages they will regard it as justification to carry on, and this is what we need, it's all part of the increase in energy levels. For those whose mission is to save the earth, they will become angered by this behavior and try even harder, and more of their emotions will be poured into her. These messages will resonate with everyone at a soul level and will only amplify what they are already doing, which can only be a good thing. This is an amazing time, people are living and fulfilling their soul purpose. They need to be empowered with these messages to remove their fear.

Is the message still very much that everything is just as it should be?

Very much so, and if something is missing things will be set in motion that will help it to manifest. We learn as we go along as well, nothing is set in stone. As things change we adapt just like you adapt. So at this very moment in time everything is perfect. Even if things might be perceived to be wicked or evil or other such words that are often used, nothing has been corrupted, and that is a significant difference from last time.

Are there really any forces or entities that can be thought of as negative or operating 'outside the plan'?

There is negative but nothing outside of the plan, as with any environment that has duality. Even the council has both negative and positive if you want to use those terms, and it is the soul memories of these things that are deep within us that have given rise to the references to all this found in various religions. They all have gods and devils, heavens and hells, that's simply the dualistic perception of it all. But this darker side is just as needed in the world.

So nothing is outside of the plan?

No.

And there are no 'demonic forces' trying to 'subvert the course of righteousness'?

People who suggest that are fighting their own battle. They resonate with it because they have their own inner struggle with opposing forces, and they are projecting it onto something else.

So they are externalizing something that is really internal?

Yes.

universal excitement over this unique opportunity

Is this the first time this kind of opportunity has ever arisen in the history of the universe?

It's difficult to explain, because it's not the first time, but for the vibration or level that we all work on it is. There are different changes on different scales going on the whole time. But this, even in our eyes, is on a very grand scale.

What's the purpose of not having a certain outcome this time round?

New experiences will be born out of it that even we haven't conceived yet. The spiritual awakening that is happening globally is like a baby opening its eyes for the first time. We decided this time to give a glimpse of eternity to people. This is one of the reasons why it's so exciting at this time. Never before have you had the chance to be in a body but also see eternity. How amazing that is!

And we are watching to see how this will help you to grow and shift without people using it in a way that is wasn't meant for. This is why we're so excited this time round. It's not by chance that you can now see what you can see. But we know that this is necessary for the changes that need

111

to be put into place, so that the veil of fear can be lifted for the majority rather than the minority.

Do you have any final messages for us?

When you can see past what goes on immediately around you, the excitement for change is incredible! If you could feel what we feel! It is exciting for us to be able to be involved, and to be heard in your lives. This is a first. This we did not do the last time, and we're learning from it. And your group is just one of many. This is happening all over. And if we can instill anything in you it's the excitement of the culmination of this process, of why you have chosen to be here.

SESSION 2

Do you have any further positive messages that will reinforce our sense of excitement about this unique opportunity?

You may think of the earth like a caterpillar. All this time it's been growing, and for the last few thousand years it's almost like it's been in a cocoon, while all these souls have been playing out their roles on it. And now a butterfly is emerging. That is the best way to think of how the earth will be after the shift. This beautiful thing.

And just like the caterpillar couldn't fly before and now it can, this energy will bring through new qualities, new things that can be done, new experiences, the earth will have another dimension to it. And the people on it will experience that dimension. There will be better communication. There will be better understanding. It will be a more gentle place to live. Duality will still remain but people will be more comfortable with the middle ground.

Do you have any more final messages for us?

Many of you have waited many, many years and even lifetimes to get to this point. And it's a shame that so many of you have waited so long, and yet now you're nearly there you don't have the excitement and enthusiasm, but have fear instead. The most important thing to remember is that you have chosen this because it is an incredible journey! And an expansion you would not have experienced in a physical body before, or at least not for a very long time.

So these are exciting possibilities that we should be looking forward to...

YES!

Other Books by Ian Lawton

published by Rational Spirituality Press *www.rspress.org*

YOUR HOLOGRAPHIC SOUL This is a short, simple pocket book, written in a question-and-answer style. It tackles seven key questions to build a Rational Spiritual framework, and then offers ten self-help suggestions for how we can use it to get the most out of our day-to-day lives.

THE LITTLE BOOK OF THE SOUL This is a short, simple pocket book, written in a story-book style. It contains a selection of the most interesting near-death and past-life cases that support Rational Spirituality, interspersed with simple summaries and analysis.

THE BIG BOOK OF THE SOUL This is the main reference book for Rational Spirituality, written in a relatively academic style. It contains full details of key cases, in-depth analysis of all key topics and full source references.

THE HISTORY OF THE SOUL This is a lengthy, relatively academic book that explores the texts and traditions from around the world that discuss the previous shifts and the reasons for them.

IAN LAWTON was born in 1959. In his mid-thirties he became a writer-researcher specializing in ancient history, esoterica and spiritual philosophy. His first two books, *Giza: The Truth* (1999) and *Genesis Unveiled* (2003), have sold over 30,000 copies worldwide.

In *The Book of the Soul* (2004) he developed the idea of Rational Spirituality, also establishing himself as one of the world's leading authorities on the interlife. And in *The Wisdom of the Soul* (2007) he first introduced the idea of the holographic soul. His other books include *The Little Book of the Soul* (2007), *The Big Book of the Soul* (2008, a complete rewrite of the 2004 book), *Your Holographic Soul* (2010), *The Future of the Soul* (2010) and *The History of the Soul* (2010, a revision of the 2003 book). For further information see *www.ianlawton.com*.

He is also a practicing regression therapist, training with the Past Life Regression Academy (PLRA). See *www.regressionacademy.com*.

JANET TRELOAR saw and communicated with spirits from an early age. She chose to repress this natural ability as she got older but, after many years working in the corporate sector, various synchronicities led her to rediscover it. Now as a graduate of the

PLRA she has a private regression therapy practice operating out of Woodford Green and Central London, with spirit release work as one of her specialisms. This is her first major foray into channeling, and she is now undertaking further research on 2012 with Tracey. She also hopes to emigrate to Vancouver at some stage to set up a PLRA affiliated regression training centre. For more information see *www.planet-therapies.com*.

HAZEL NEWTON is the co-director of the PLRA. She has a private regression therapy practice in Bristol, specializing in soul contracts and healing

 the inner child. She also runs basic and advanced hypnosis classes, is currently co-authoring a book to be called *Rational Reincarnation* with Peter Jenkins and Toni Ann Winninger, and writes a monthly column for *www.mastersofthespiritworld.com*. For more information see *www.radiantsouls.co.uk*.

TRACEY ROBINS was born in Melbourne, Australia and is privileged to have traveled widely.

 As a graduate of the PLRA she has established a private regression therapy practice in Manchester. She is currently undertaking further research on 2012 with Janet, and hopes to return to Australia at some stage to set up a PLRA affiliated regression training centre. For more information see *www.lifecycletherapies.com*.